E. Lynn Linton

About Ireland

E. Lynn Linton

About Ireland

ISBN/EAN: 9783337324810

Printed in Europe, USA, Canada, Australia, Japan

Cover: Foto ©Andreas Hilbeck / pixelio.de

More available books at **www.hansebooks.com**

BY

E. LYNN LINTON

SECOND EDITION

LONDON
METHUEN & CO.
18, BURY STREET, W.C.
1890

EXPLANATORY.

I AM conscious that I ought to make some kind of apology for rushing into print on a subject which I do not half know. But I do know just a little more than I did when I was an ardent Home Ruler, influenced by the seductive charm of sentiment and abstract principle only; and I think that perhaps the process by which my own blindness has been couched may help to clear the vision of others who see as I did. All of us lay-folk are obliged to follow the leaders of those schools in politics, science, or religion, to which our temperament and mental idiosyncracies affiliate us. Life is not long enough for us to examine from the beginning upwards all the questions in which we are interested; and it is only by chance that we find ourselves set face to face with the first principles and elemental facts of a cause to which, perhaps, as blind and believing followers of our leaders, we have committed ourselves with the ardour of conviction and the intemperance of ignorance. In this matter of Ireland I believed in the accusations of brutality, injustice, and general insolence of tyranny from modern landlords to existing tenants, so constantly made by the Home Rulers and their organs; and, shocking though the undeniable crimes committed by the Campaigners were, they seemed to me the tragic results of that kind of

despair which seizes on men who, goaded to madness
by oppression, are reduced to masked murder as their
sole means of defence—and as, after all, but a sadly
natural retaliation. I knew nothing really of Lord
Ashbourne's Act; and what I thought I knew was,
that it was more a blind than honest legislation, and
did no vital good. I thought that Home Rule would
set all things straight, and that the National Sentiment
was one which ought to find practical expression. I
rejoiced over every election that took away one seat
from the Unionists and added another vote to the
Home Rulers; and I shut my eyes to the dismember-
ment of our glorious Empire and the certainty of
civil war in Ireland, should the Home Rule demanded
by the Parnellites and advocated by the Gladstonians
become an accomplished fact. In a word I committed
the mistakes inevitable to all who take feeling and
conviction rather than fact and knowledge for their
guides.

Then I went to Ireland; and the scales fell from my
eyes. I saw for myself; heard facts I had never known
before; and was consequently enlightened as to the
true meaning of the agitation and the real condition of
the people in their relation to politics, their landlords,
and the Plan of Campaign.

The outcome of this visit was two papers which
were written for the *New Review*—with the editor of
whom, however, I stood somewhat in the position of
Balaam with Balak, when, called on to curse the
Israelites, he was forced by a superior power to bless
them. So I with the Unionists. The first paper was
sent and passed, but it was delayed by editorial diffi-

culties through the critical months of the bye-elections.
When published in the December number, owing to
the exigencies of space, the backbone—namely the
extracts from the Land Acts, now included in this
re-publication—was taken out of it, and my own
unsupported statements alone were left.   I was sorry
for this, as it cut the ground from under my feet
and left me in the position of one of those mere
impressionists who have already sufficiently darkened
counsel and obscured the truth of things.   As the
same editorial difficulties and exigencies of space
would doubtless delay the second paper, like the first,
I resolved, by the courteous permission of the editor,
to enlarge and publish both in a pamphlet for which I
alone should be responsible, and which would bind no
editor to even the semblance of endorsement.

I, only half-enlightened, write, as has been said, for
the wholly blind and ignorantly ardent who, as I did,
accept sentiment for fact and feeling for demonstration ;
who do not look at the solid legal basis on which the
present Government is dealing with the Irish question ;
who believe all that the Home Rulers say, and
nothing that the Unionists demonstrate.   I want them
to study the plain and indisputable facts of legislation
as I have done, when I think they must come to the
same conclusions as those which have forced themselves on my own mind—namely, that the Home Rule
desired by the Parnellites is not only a delusive impossibility, but is also high treason against the integrity of
the Empire, and would be a base surrender of our
obligations to the Irish Loyalists ; that, whatever the
landlords were, they are now more sinned against than

sinning; and that in the orderly operation of the Land Acts now in force, with the stern repression of outrages * and punishment of crimes, for which peaceable folk are so largely indebted to Mr. Balfour, lies the true pacification of this distressed and troubled country.

E. LYNN LINTON.

---

* Lord Hartington's statistics—and Lord Hartington is a man whose word not his bitterest enemies have dared to question or to doubt—are these:

1880 (No coercion) .. .. 2,585 agrarian crimes.
1881 (Partial and weak coercion) 4,439 ., ,,
1883 (Vigorous coercion) .. 834 ., .,
1888 (Vigorous coercion) .. 660 ., .,

ABOUT IRELAND.

NOTHING dies so hard as prejudice, unless it be sentiment. Indeed, prejudice and sentiment are but different manifestations of the same principle by which men pronounce on things according to individual feeling, independent of facts and free from the restraint of positive knowledge. And on nothing in modern times has so much sentiment been lavished as on the Irish question; nowhere has so much passionately generous, but at the same time so much absolutely ignorant, partisanship been displayed as by English sympathisers with the Irish peasant. This is scarcely to be wondered at. The picture of a gallant nation ground under the heel of an iron despotism—of an industrious and virtuous peasantry rackrented, despoiled, brutalised, and scarce able to live by their labour that they may supply the vicious wants of oppressive landlords—of unarmed men, together with women and little children, ruthlessly bludgeoned by a brutal police, or shot by a bloodthirsty soldiery for no greater offence than verbal protests against illegal evictions—of a handful of ardent patriots ready to undergo imprisonment and contumely in their struggle against one of the strongest nations in the world for only so much political freedom as is granted to-day by despots themselves—such a picture as this is calculated to excite the sympathies of all generous souls. And it has done so in England, where "Home Rule" and "Justice to Ireland" have become the rallying cries of one section of the Liberal party, to the disruption and political suicide of the whole body ; and where the less know-ledge imported into the question the more fervid the advocacy and the louder the demand.

It is worth while to state quite quietly and quite plainly how things stand at this present moment. There is no need for hysterics on the one side or the other ; and to amend one's views by the testimony of facts is not a dishonest turning of one's coat—if con-fession of that amendment is a little like the white sheet and lighted taper of a penitent. Things are, or they are not. If they are, as will be set down, the inference is plain to anyone not hopelessly blinded by preconceived prejudice. If they are not, let them be authoritatively contradicted on the basis of fact, not sentiment—demonstration, not assertion. In any case it is a gain to obtain material for a truer judgment than heretofore, and thus to be rid of certain mental films by which colours are blurred and perspective is distorted.

No one wishes to palliate the crimes of which England has been guilty in Ireland. Her hand has been heavy, her whip one of braided scorpions, her rule emphatically of blood and iron. But all this is of the past, and the pendulum, not only of public feeling but of legal enactment, threatens to swing too far on the other side. What has been done cannot be undone, but it will not be repeated. We shall never send over another Cromwell nor yet another Castlereagh; and there is as little good to be got from chafing over past wrongs as there is in lamenting past glories. Malachi and his collar of gold—the ancient kings who led forth the Red Branch Knights—State persecution of the Catholics—rack-rents and unjust evictions, are all alike swept away into the limbo of things dead and done with. What Ireland has to deal with now are the enactments and facts of the day, and to shake off the incubus of retrospection, as a strong man awaking would get rid of a nightmare.

Nowhere in Europe, nor yet in the United States, are tenant-farmers so well protected by law as in Ireland; nor is it the fault of England if the Acts passed for their benefit have been rendered ineffectual by the agitators who have preferred fighting to orderly development. So long ago as 1860 a Bill was passed providing that no tenant should be evicted for non-payment of rent unless one year's rent in arrear. (Landlord and Tenant Act, 1860, sec. 52.) Even then, when evicted, he could recover possession within six months by payment of the amount due; when the landlord had to pay him the amount of any profit he had made out of the lands in the interim. The landlord had to pay half the poor rate of the Government Valuation if a holding was £4 or upward, and all the poor rate if it was under £4. By the Act of 1870 " a yearly tenant disturbed in his holding by the act of the landlord, for causes other than non-payment of rent, and the Government Valuation of whose holding does not exceed £100 per annum, must be paid by his

landlord not only full compensation for all improvements made by himself or his predecessors, such as
unexhausted manures, permanent buildings, and
reclamation of waste lands, but also as compensation
for disturbance, a sum of money which may amount to
seven years' rent." (Land Act of 1870, secs. 1, 2, and 3.)
Under the Act of 1881 the landlord's power of disturbance was practically abolished—but I think I have
read somewhere that even of late years, and with the
ballot, certain landlords in England have threatened
their tenants with " disturbance " without compensation if their votes were not given to the right colour
—while in Ireland, even when evicted for non-payment of rent, a yearly tenant must be paid by
his landlord " compensation for all improvements,
such as unexhausted manures, permanent buildings,
and reclamation of waste land." (Sec. 4.) And when
his rent does not exceed £15 he must be paid in addition
" a sum of money which may amount to seven years'
rent if the court decides that the rent is exorbitant."
(Secs. 3 and 9.) (a) Until the contrary is proved, the
improvements are presumed to have been made by the
tenants. (Sec. 5.) (b) The tenant can make his claim
for compensation immediately on notice to quit being
served, and cannot be evicted until the compensation
is paid. (Secs. 16 and 21.) A yearly tenant when
voluntarily surrendering his farm must either be paid
by the landlord (a) compensation for all his improvements, or (b) be permitted to sell his improvements to
an incoming tenant. (Sec. 4.) In all new tenancies
the landlord must pay half the county or Grand Jury
Cess if the valuation is £4 or upward and the whole

of the same Cess if the value does not exceed £4. (Secs. 65 and 66.) Thus we have under the Land Act of 1870 (1) Full payment for all improvements; (2) Compensation for disturbance.

The famous Land Act of 1881 gave three additional privileges. (1) Fixity of tenure, by which the tenant remains in possession of the land for ever, subject to periodic revision of the rent. (Land Act, 1881, sec. 8.) If the tenant has not had a fair rent fixed, and his landlord proceeds to evict him for non-payment of rent, he can apply to the court to fix the fair rent, and meantime the eviction proceedings will be restrained by the court. (Sec. 13.) (2) Fair rent, by which any yearly tenant may apply to the Land Commission Court (the judges of which were appointed under Mr. Gladstone's Administration) to fix the fair rent of his holding. The application is referred to three persons, one of whom is a lawyer, and the other two inspect and value the farm. *This rent can never again* be raised by the landlord. (Sec. 8.) (3) Free sale, by which every yearly tenant may, whether he has had a fair rent fixed or not, sell his tenancy to the highest bidder whenever he desires to leave. (Sec. 1.) (*a*) There is no practical limit to the price he may sell for, and twenty times the amount of the annual rent has frequently been obtained in every province of Ireland. (*b*) Even if a tenant be evicted, he has the right either to redeem at any time within three months, *or to sell his tenancy within the same period to a purchaser who can likewise redeem* and thus acquire all the privileges of a tenant. (Sec. 13.)

Even more important than this is the Land Purchase Act of 1885, commonly called Lord Ashbourne's Act,

by which the whole land in Ireland is potentially put
into the hands of the farmers, and of the working of
which much will have to be said before these papers
end. This Act, in its sections 2, 3, and 4, sets forth
this position, briefly stated : If a tenant wishes to buy
his holding, and arranges with his landlord as to terms,
he can change his position from that of a perpetual
rent-payer into that of the payer of an annuity,
terminable at the end of forty-nine years—the
Government supplying him with the entire purchase-
money, to be repaid during those forty-nine years at
4 per cent. This annual payment of £4 for every £100
borrowed covers both principal and interest. Thus,
if a tenant, already paying a statutory rent of £50,
agrees to buy from his landlord at twenty years' purchase (or £1,000) the Government will lend him the
money, his rent will at once cease, and he will not pay
£50, but £40, yearly for forty-nine years, and then
become the owner of his holding, free of rent. It is
hardly necessary to point out that, as these forty-nine
years of payment roll by, the interest of the tenant in
his holding increases rapidly in value. (Land Purchase
Act, 1885, secs. 2, 3, and 4.)

Under the Land Act of 1887, the tenants received
the following still greater and always one-sided privileges.
(1) By this Act leases are allowed to be broken by the
tenant, but not by the landlord. All leaseholders
whose leases would expire within ninety-nine years
after the passing of the Act have the option of going
into court and getting their contracts broken and a
judicial rent fixed. No equivalent power is given to the
landlords. (Land Act of 1887, secs. 1 and 2.) (2) The

Act varies rent already judicially fixed for fifteen years by the Land Courts in the years 1881, 1882, 1883, 1884, and 1885. (Sec. 29.) (3) It stays evictions, and allows rent to be paid by instalments. In the case of tenants whose valuation does not exceed £50, the court before which proceedings are being taken for the recovery of *any* debt due by the tenant is empowered to stay his eviction, and may give him liberty to pay his creditors by instalments, and can extend the time for such payment as it thinks proper. (Land Act of 1887, sec. 30.)

By these extracts, which do not exhaust the whole of the privileges granted to the Irish tenant, it may be seen how exceptionally he has been favoured. Nowhere else has such wholesale interference with the obligations of contract, such lavish protection of the tenant, such practical persecution of the landlord been as yet demanded by the one-half of the nation ; nor, if demanded, would such partiality have been conceded by the other half. Yet, in the face of these various Acts, and all they embody, provide for, and deny, our hysterical journal *par excellence* is not ashamed to publish a wild letter from one of those ramping political women who screech like peacocks before rain, setting forth how Ireland could be redeemed by the manufacture of blackberry jam, were it not for the infamous landlords who would at once raise the rent on those tenants who, by industry, had improved their condition. And a Dublin paper asserts that anything will be fiction which demonstrates that " Ireland is not the home of rackrenters, brutal batonmen, and heartless evictors " ; while political agitation is still being carried on by any means that come handiest, and the eviction of tenants who owe five or six years' rent, and will not pay even one to clear off old scores, is treated as an act of brutality for which no quarter should be given. If we were to transfer the whole method of procedure to our own lands and houses in England, perhaps the thing would wear a different aspect from that which it wears now, when surrounded by a halo of false sentiment and convenient forgetfulness.

The total want of honesty, of desire for the right thing in this no-rent agitation, is exemplified by the following fact :—When Colonel Vandeleur's tenants—owing several years' rent, refused to pay anything, and joined the Plan of Campaign, arbitration was suggested, and Sir Charles Russell was accepted by the landlord as arbitrator. As every one knows, Sir Charles is an Irishman, a Catholic, and the "tenants' friend." His award was, as might have been expected, most liberal towards them. Here is the result :—" We learn that the non-fulfilment by a number of the tenants of the terms of the award made by Sir C. Russell is likely to lead to serious difficulties. They refuse to carry out the undertaking which was given on their behalf, having so much bettered the instruction given to them that they insist upon holding a grip of the rent, and not yielding to even the advice of their friends. About thirty of them have not paid the year's rent, which all the Plan of Campaign tenants were to have paid when the award was made known to them. This is the most conspicuous instance in which arbitration has been tried, and the result is not encouraging, although landlords have been denounced for not at once accepting it instead of seeking to enforce their legal rights by the tribunal appointed by the Legislature."

With a legal machinery of relief so comprehensive and so favourable to the tenant, it would seem that the Plan of Campaign, with its cruel and murderous accompaniments, was scarcely needed. If anyone was aggrieved, the courts were open to him ; and we have only to read the list of reduced rents to see how those courts protected the tenant and bore heavily on the landlord. Also, it would seem to persons of ordinary morality that it would have been more manly and more honest to pay the rents due to the proprietor than to cast the money into the chest of the Plan of Campaign—that *boîte à Pierrette* which, like the sieve of the Danaïdes, can never be filled. The Home Rule agitators have known how to make it appear that they, and they alone, stand between the people and oppression. They have ignored all this orderly legal machinery ; and their English sympathisers have not remembered it. Nor have those English sympathisers considered the significant fact that this agitation is literally the bread of life to those who have created and still maintain it. Many of the Home Rule Irish Members of Parliament have risen from the lowest ranks of society—from the barefooted peasantry, where their nearest relations are still to be found—into the outward condition of gentlemen living in comparative affluence. It is not being uncharitable, nor going behind motives, to ask, *Cui bono ?* For whose advantage is a certain movement carried on ?— especially for whose advantage is this anti-rent movement in Ireland ? For the good of the tenants who, under the pressure put on them by those whom they

have agreed to follow, refuse to pay even a fraction of
rent hitherto paid to the full, and who are, in consequence, evicted from their farms and deprived of their
means of subsistence?—or is it for the good of a handful
of men who live by and on the agitation they created and
still keep up? Do the leaders of any movement what-
soever give a thought to the individual lives sacrificed to
the success of the cause? As little as the general regrets
the individuals of the rank and file in the battalions he
hurls against the enemy. The ruined homes and blighted
lives of the thousands who have listened, believed, been
coerced to their own despair, have been no more than
the numbers of the rank and file to the general who hoped
to gain the day by his battalions.* The good in this
no-rent movement is reaped by the agitators alone ;
and for them alone have the chestnuts been pulled
out of the fire. Furthermore, whose hands among
the prominent leaders are free from the reflected
stain of blood-money? These leaders have counselled
a course of action which has been marked all along the
line by outrage and murder ; and they have lived well
and amassed wealth by the course they have counselled.

---

* Mr. Hurlbert, a Roman Catholic, an American, and a personal
friend of Mr. Davitt—all which circumstances give a special weight
to his testimony, now borne after frequent and lengthened and recent
visits to Ireland, and after close converse with men of all classes and
of all political and religious views, says in his *Ireland under Coercion :*
" An Irish gentleman from St. Louis brought over a considerable
sum of money for the relief of distress in the north-west of Ireland,
but was induced to entrust it to the League, on the express ground
that, the more people were made to feel the pinch of the existing
order of things, the better it would be for the revolutionary movement."—*The Irish Question*, I., 193. By Dr. Bryce.

From proletariats in their own persons they have become men of substance and property. These assertions are facts to which names and amounts can be given ; and that question, *Cui bono?* answers itself. The inference to be drawn is too grave to be set aside ; and to plead "charitable judgment" is to plead imbecility.

The plain and simple truth is—the protective legislation that was so sorely needed for the peasantry is fast degenerating into injustice and oppression against the landlords. Thousands of the smaller landowners have been absolutely beggared ; the larger holders have been as ruthlessly ruined. For, while the rents were lowered, the charges on the land, made on the larger basis, were kept to their same value ; and the fate of the landlord was sealed. Between the hammer and the anvil as he was and is placed, his times have not been pleasant. Families who have bought their estates on the faith of Government sales and Government contracts, and families who have owned theirs for centuries and lived on them, winter and summer—who have been neither absentees nor rack-renters, but have been friendly, hospitable, open-handed after their kind, always ready to give comforts and medicine to the sick and a good-natured measure of relief to the hard pressed—they have now been brought to the ground ; and between our own fluid and unstable legislation and the reckless cruelty of the Plan of Campaign their destruction has been complete. Wherever one goes one finds great houses shut up or let for a few summer months to strangers who care nothing for the place and less than nothing for the people. One cannot call this a gain, look at it as one will. Nor do the tenantry themselves feel it to be a gain. Get their confidence and you will find that they all regret the loss of their own—those jovial, frank, and kindly proprietors who did the best they knew, though perhaps, judged by present scientific knowledge that best was not very good, but who at least knew more than themselves. Carrying the thing home to England, we should scarcely say that our country places would be the better for the exodus of all the educated and refined and well-to-do families, with the peasantry and an unmarried clergyman left sole masters of the situation.

In the desire of Parliament to do justice to the Irish peasant, whose condition did once so loudly demand amelioration, justice to the landlord has gone by the board. For we cannot call it justice to make him alone suffer. His rents have been reduced from 25 to 30 per cent. and over, but all the rent charges, mortgages, debts and dues have been retained at their full value. The scheme of reduction does not pass beyond the tiller of the soil, and the landlord is the sole loser.*

---

* Some time after the Great Famine, the Government brought in an Act called the Encumbered Estates Act. A judge was appointed to act as auctioneer. The income of the estate was set out in schedule form, and a man purchased that income by competition in open court. He got with his purchase what was supposed to be the best title then known, commonly called "A Parliamentary title." If he wanted to sell again, that was enough. Many years after the bargain was made by the court, Mr. Gladstone dropped in and upset it. A friend of mind purchased a guaranteed rental of £600 a year, subject to £300 annuity, as well as other charges, head rent, &c., &c. Now the Government may have been said to have pledged its honour to him, speaking by the mouth of a judge in open court, that it was

Beyond this he suffers from the want of finality in legislation. Nothing is left to prove itself, and the tinkering never ends. A fifteen years' bargain under the first Land Act is broken up under the next as if Governmental pledges were lovers' vows. When, on the faith of those pledges, a landlord borrowed money from the Board of Works for the improvement of his estate, for stone cottages for his tenantry, for fences, drainage, and the like, suddenly his income is still further reduced ; but the interest he has to pay for the loan contracted on the broader basis remains the same. Which is a kind of thing on all fours with the plan of locking up a debtor so that he cannot work at his trade, while ordering him to pay so much weekly from earnings which the law itself prevents his making.

If the sum of misery remains constant in Ireland, its distribution has changed hands. The small deposits in the savings-banks have increased to an enormous extent, and in many places where the tenants have for

---

selling him £600 a year. Surely it was a distinct breach of faith to swoop down on the purchaser, years after, and reduce the £600 to £500 without reducing the charges also in due proportion, or giving back one-sixth of the purchase money. Mr. Gladstone and his party say the land was rented too high. Does that (if true) get over the dishonesty of selling for £600 a year what was really worth only 500 ? Such a transaction as that between man and man would be actionable as a fraud. But this excuse is not true, for when any tenant wants to sell his tenant-right he gets a large price for it, far larger than the normal proportion to his rent. When a nation sanctions such absolute dishonesty as this on the part of its Prime Minister, it is not surprising that the shrewd Irish peasant profits by the lesson and improves the example.

some years refused to pay their rents, but have still kept the land, the women have learned to dress. But the owners of the land—say that they are ladies with no man in the family—have wanted bread, and have been kept from starvation only by surreptitious supplies delivered in the dead darkness of the night. These supplies have of necessity been rare and scanty, for the most honest tenant dared not face the vengeance of the League by openly paying his just due. Did not Mr. Dillon, on August 23rd, 1887, say, " If there is a man in Ireland base enough to back down, to turn his back on the fight now that Coercion has passed, I pledge myself in the face of this meeting, that I will denounce him from public platform by name, and I pledge myself to the Government that, let that man be whom he may, his life will not be a happy one, either in Ireland or across the seas." With such a formidable organisation as this, what individual would have the courage to stand out for abstract justice to a landlord? It would have been, and it has been, standing out for his own destruction. Hence, for no fault, no rack-renting, have proprietors— and especially ladies—been treated as mortal enemies by those whom they had always befriended—for no reason whatever but that it was an easy victory for the Campaigners to obtain. Women, with never a man to defend them, could be more easily manipulated than if they were so many stalwart young fellows, handy in their turn with guns and revolvers, and man for man a match even for Captain Moonlight. If these ladies dared to evict their non-paying tenants they would be either boycotted or " visited," or perhaps both. Besides, who would venture to take the vacant land? And how could a couple of delicate ladies, say, till the ground with their own hands? The old fable of the dog in the manger holds good with these Campaigners. Those who will not pay prevent others who would; and the hated " landgrabber," denounced from altar and platform alike, is simply an honest and industrious worker, who would make his own living and the landlord's rent out of a bit of land which is lying idle and going to waste.

All through the disturbed districts we come upon facts like this—upon the ruin and humiliation of kindly and delicately-nurtured ladies, of which the English public knows nothing; and while it hysterically pities the poor down-trodden peasant and goes in for Home Rule as the panacea, the wife of a tenant owing five years' rent and refusing to pay one, dresses in costly attire—and the lady proprietor knows penury and hunger; not to speak of the agonies of personal terror endured for months at a stretch. Let us, who live in a well-ordered country, realize for a moment the mental condition of those who dwell in the shadow of assassination—women to whom every unusual noise is as the sentence of death, and whose days are days of trembling, and their nights nights of anguish for the fear of death that encompasses them. Is this according to the law of elemental justice? Are our sympathies to be confined wholly to one class, and are the sorrows and the wrongs done to another not to count? Surely it is time for some of the sentimental fog in which so many of us have been living to be dispelled in favour of the light of truth!

Here is an instructive little bit on which we would do well to ponder :—

A certain authority gives the following anecdote :— He says that he "has just had a long conversation with one of the leading Galway merchants. 'A farmer of this county,' said he, 'told me yesterday that he had let his meadowing at £8 an acre. I bought all his barley, and he confessed that on this crop too he had made £8 an acre. Now the judicial rent of this man's holding is 10s. the acre. He said, "I have nothing to complain of."' This man was a tenant of Lord Clanricarde; one of those people who decline to pay a farthing in the way of rent to the lawful owner of the soil. The case we have cited may be an extreme one, but it is generally admitted by those who are acquainted with the facts, and who speak the truth that the rents on the Clanricarde property, speaking generally, are low rents, and yet not only is it impossible to collect these rents, but the agent who represents Lord Clanricarde, and whose only fault is that he tries to do his duty to his employer without unnecessary harshness to the tenantry, dare not go outside his house without an escort of police, and every time he leaves his house, he risks his life. Referring to this agent, Mr. Tener, the correspondent says :—

"No one would think from looking at him that he literally carries his life in his hand, and that if he were not guarded as closely as he is he would be shot in twenty-four hours. He never goes outside the walls of the Portumna demesne without an escort of seven police-men—two mounted men in front, two behind, and three upon his car. He, too, as well as the driver, is armed,

So the would-be assassins must reckon with nine
armed men. In the opinion of those who know the
neighbourhood his escort is barely strong enough. He
was fired at a few weeks ago, and the horse which he was
driving shot dead. The police who were with him on
the car were rolled out upon the road, and before they
could recover themselves and pursue the Moonlighters
had escaped.' And this is supposed to be a civilised
country, and is a part of the United Kingdom !

" Whereas it seems to us Lord Clanricarde is to blame
is in not living, at any rate for some part of the year,
upon his Irish property. This nobleman represents
one of the most ancient families in Ireland. He is
the representative of the Clanricarde Burkes, who
have been settled upon this property for 700 years.
He draws, or rather drew, a very large income from it,
and there can be little question that his presence
would encourage and sustain smaller proprietors who
are fighting a losing battle in defence of their rights.
These proprietors may fairly claim that the leading
men of their order should stand by them in the time of
trial. Unfortunately, this assistance has not been
invariably, or even as a rule, rendered by the great
Irish landowners. It is, indeed, largely because they
have failed in their duty that the present troubles have
come upon Irish landlords as a body. If only in the
past the great landowners had lived in Ireland and
spent at least a portion of the incomes they derived from
Ireland upon their estates, the present agitation against
landlordism would never have reached the point at
which it has arrived. The absence of the landlords,
and in many cases their refusal to recognise the legiti-

mate claims of their districts upon them, has made it possible for the agitators who have now the ear of the people to bring about that severance of classes, and that embittered feeling of class against class, whic is doing Ireland more injury at the present time than all the rack-renters put together."

Those who plead for the landlords who have been so cruelly robbed and ruined are weak-voiced and reticent compared to the loudly crying advocates for the peasantry. English tourists run over for a fortnight to Ireland, talk to the jarvies, listen to the peasants themselves, forbear to go near any educated or responsible person with knowledge of the facts and a character to lose, and accept as gospel everything they hear. There is no check and no verification. Pat and Tim and Mike give their accounts of this and that, bedad! and tell their piteous tales of want and oppression. The English tourist swallows it all whole as it comes to him, and writes his account to the sympathetic Press, which publishes as gospel stories which have not one word of truth in them. In fact, the term " English tourist " has come to mean the same as *gobemouche* in France; and clever Pat knows well enough that there is not a fly in the whole region of fable which is too large for the brutal Saxon to swallow. Abject poverty without shoes to its feet, with only a few rags to cover its unwashed nakedness, and an unfurnished mud cabin shared with the pigs and poultry for its sole dwelling-place—abject poverty begs a copper from " his honour" for the love of God and the glory of the Blessed Virgin, telling meantime a heartrending story of privation and oppression. Abject poverty points to all the outward signs and circumstances of its woe; but it forgets the good stone house in which live the son and the son's wife—the dozen or more of cattle grazing free on the mountain side—that bit of fertile land where the very weeds grow into beauty by their luxuriance—and those quiet hundreds hidden away for the sole pleasure of hoarding. And the English tourist takes it all in, and blazes out into wrath against the tyrannous landlord who has reduced an honest citizen to this fearful state of misery; knowing nothing of the craft which is known to all the residents round about, and not willing to believe it were he even told. For the dramatic instinct is strong in human nature, and in these later days there is an ebullient surplusage of sympathy which only desires to find an object. Across the Bristol Channel, the English tourist finds these objects ready-made to his hand; and the question is still further embroiled, and the light of truth still more obscured, that a few impulsive, credulous, and non-judicially-minded young people may find something whereon to excite their emotions, and give vent to them in letters to the newspapers when excited.

Only the other day a young Irishman who has to do with the land question was mistaken for a brutal but credulous Saxon by the jarvey who had him in tow. Consequently, Pat plied his fancied victim with the wildest stories of this man's wrongs and that lone widow's sufferings. When he found out his mistake he laughed and said: "Begorra, I thought your honour was an English tourist!" And at a certain trial which took place in Cork, the judge put by some absurd statement by saying, half-indignant, half amused: "Do you take me for an English tourist?" Nevertheless the race will continue so long as there are excitable young persons of either sex whose capacity for swallowing flies is practically unlimited, and an hysterical Press to which they can betake themselves.

The following authoritative instance of this misplaced sympathy may suffice. The *Westminster Review* published a certain article on the Olphert estate, among other things. Those who have read it know its sensational character. At Cork the other day the priest concerned had to confess on oath that only three of the Olphert tenants had received relief.*

In the famous Luggacurren evictions the poor dispossessed dupes lost their all at the bidding of the Campaigners, on the plea of inability to pay rents voluntarily offered by Lord Lansdowne to be reduced 20 per cent. After these evictions the lands were let to the "Land Corporation," which had some short time ago four hundred head of cattle over and above the full rent paid honestly down; but the former holders are living on charity doled out to them by the Campaigners, and in huts built for them by

* The following in reference to the Olphert estate evictions under the Plan of Campaign is from the *Freeman's Journal*. Will Mr. Spencer when exhibiting his photos. state the facts about this case—which reason and common-sense show to be altogether in the landlord's favour?

"Mr. Spencer, Trowbridge, England, arrived in Falcarragh to-day, visited the scenes of the late evictions, and took photographs of several of the demolished houses in the townland of Drumnatinny. Mr. Spencer intends, on his return to England, to bring home to the minds of the English people by a series of illustrative lectures, the misery and hardships to which the Irish peasantry are subjected."

the Campaigners on the edge of the rich and kindly land which once gave them home and sustenance. How bitterly they curse the evil counsels which led to their destruction only they and the few they dare trust know. Take. too. these two authoritative stories. They are of the things one blindly believes and rages against—with what justice the dénouement of the sorry farce, best shows :—

" The correspondents of the *Freeman's Journal*, in response to the circular some time ago addressed to them continue to supply fictitious and exaggerated statements of events alleged to have happened ' in the country,' nearly every day some example is afforded. One of the latest is a pathetic tale of the ' suicide of a tenant.' It represents that Andrew Kelly, of Cloon- laugh, ' one of the three tenants against whom A. W. Sampey, J.P., landlord, obtained ejectments,' became demented from the fear of eviction, and drowned himself in a bog hole in consequence. The account is a gross misrepresentation of the facts. Andrew Kelly was not a tenant of Mr. Sampey's, nor had he been for the last five years. His son, it is true, is one of the tenants against whom a decree was obtained, but this did not apparently trouble the father much, as he had been living away from his son for a long time, although he had come to see him a few days before he was drowned. There was no suspicion either of foul play or suicide, and the coroner's jury returned no such verdict as that given in the *Freeman*. The veracious correspondent of that journal stated that the jury found that ' Andrew Kelly came by his death through drown- ing on the 22nd October while suffering under temporary insanity brought about by fear of eviction.' The following is the verdict which the coroner's jury actually arrived at :—' We find that Andrew Kelly's death was caused by suffocation ; that he was found dead in the townland of Clooncrur, on the 24th day of October, 1889.' This is the way in which sensational news is manufactured for the purpose of promoting an anti-landlord crusade and prejudicing the owners of property in the eyes of the country."

" Speaking at Newmarch, near Barnsley, last month, Mr. Waddy drew a heartrending picture of the tyranny practised in Ireland, and illustrated his theme and moved his audience to the execration of Mr. Balfour by the artistic recital of a horrible tale. He declared that a little child had been barbarously sentenced by resident magistrates to a month's imprisonment for throwing a stone at a policeman. Some hard-headed or hard-hearted Yorkshireman, however, would not believe Mr. Waddy offhand, and challenged him to declare names, place, and date. On the 15th of November, Mr. Waddy gave the following particulars in writing. He stated that the magistrates who had imposed the brutal punishment were Mr. Hill and Colonel Bowlby, that the case was tried at Keenagh on the 23rd of April, 1888, that the child's name was Thomas Quin, aged nine, and that the charge was throwing stones at the police.

" The clue thus afforded has been followed up. It is grievous that cool and calculating investigation should spoil a pretty story, but here is the truth.

" On the 20th of April, before Colonel Stewart and Colonel Bowlby, resident magistrates, Thomas Quin, aged 19 years, was convicted of using intimidation towards William Nutley, in consequence of his having done an act which he had a legal right to do—viz., to evict a labourer, Michael Fegan, of Clearis, who refused to work for him. Thomas Quin was sentenced to one month's imprisonment.

"I am quite sure that Mr. Waddy will publicly acknowledge that he played upon the feelings of his hearers with a trumped-up tale of woe, but I wonder whether anything will teach the British political tourist that a great number of my countrymen unfortunately feel a genuine delight in hoaxing them.

"Your obedient servant,

"AN IRISH LIBERAL."

As for the assertion of poverty and inability to pay, so invariably made to excuse defaulting tenants, I will give these two instances to the contrary.

"Writing on behalf of Mr. Balfour to Mr. E. Bannister, of Hyde, Cheshire, Mr. George Wyndham, M.P., recounts a somewhat remarkable circumstance in connection with the position and circumstances of a tenant on Lord Kenmare's estate who declined to pay his rent on the plea of poverty:—'Irish Office, Nov. 28, 1889. Dear Sir,—In reply to your letter of the 22nd inst., I beg to inform you that I have made careful inquiries into the case of Molloy, a tenant on Lord Kenmare's estate. I find that so far from exaggerating the scope of this incident, you somewhat understate the case. The full particulars were as follow:—The estate bailiffs visited the house of Molloy, a tenant who owed

£30 rent and arrears. They seized his cows, and then
called at his home to ask him if he would redeem them
by paying the debt. Molloy stated that he was willing
to pay, but that he had only £7 altogether. He handed
seven notes to the bailiff, who found that one of them was
a £5 note, so that the amount was £11 instead of £7.
On being pressed to pay the balance he admitted that
he had a small deposit of £20 in the bank, and produced
a document which he said was the deposit receipt for
this sum. On the bailiff examining this receipt he found it
was for £100 and not for £20. On being informed of his
mistake, Molloy took back the £100 receipt and produced
another, which turned out to be for £40. A further
search on his part led to the production of the receipt
for £20, with which and £10 in notes he paid the rent.
You will observe that this tenant, refusing to pay £30,
and obliging his landlord to take steps against him,
possessed at the time £171, besides having stock on his
land.—Yours faithfully, GEORGE WYNDHAM.'"

And I have it on the word of honour of one whose
word is his bond, that certain defaulting tenants lately
confessed to him that they had in their pockets as much
as the value of three years' rent for the two they owed, but
that they dared not, for their lives, pay it. They would
if they dared, but they dared not. The plea of inability
to pay the reduced scale of rent is for the most part simple
moonshine; and the terrorism imported into this question
comes from the Campaigners, not from the landlords,
nor yet from the police. If these paid political agitators
were silenced, and if the laws already passed were suffered
to work by themselves according to their intent, things
would speedily settle. But then the agitators would

lose their means of subsistence, their social status, and their political importance. As things are these men are ruining the country they affect to defend; while the worst enemies of the peasant are those who call themselves his friends, and the blind-eyed sympathisers who bewail the wrongs he does not suffer and the misery he himself might prevent. All that Ireland wants now is rest from political agitation, the orderly development of its resources ;—and especially finality in legislation ; *— so that the one side may know to what it has to trust, and the other may be freed from those illusive dreams and demoralising hopes which destroy the manlier efforts after self-help in the present for that universal amelioration to be found in the coming of the cockli-cranes in the future.

* On this question of further legislation I will quote part of a letter from a correspondent which shows the views of a singularly able, impartial, and fair-minded Irishman. " The breaking of leases was another risky thing to do, for it shook all faith in the sovereignty of the law and the finality of its *dicta*. Till Mr. Gladstone made himself the champion of the tenants and the oppressor of the landlords, Parliament never dreamed of revising rents paid under leases. Mr. Gladstone began by breaking these leases when held for a certain term defined by him. But we cannot stop there now. If another Land Bill is to be brought in by the present Government it must, to really and finally settle matters, *break all leases.* If it stops short of this the trouble will crop up again. If a man now with a thirty-nine years' lease can go into the Land Court, the man with a lease of a hundred years, or a hundred and fifty, or two hundred, should not be shut out. This point cannot be put too strongly to this Government. If the thing is to be done let it be done thoroughly, and let every man who holds a lease—no matter for what term—go into the Land Court, and also purchase under Lord Ashbourne's Act. Lord Ashbourne's Act is the real cure if made to apply all round."

There is, however, a good work quietly going on which will touch the evil root of things in time, but not in the sense of the Home Rulers and Campaigners. This good work will render it unnecessary to follow the advice of that rough and ready politician who saw no way out of the wood save to " send to Hell for Oliver Cromwell "; also that of the facetious Dove who winked as he offered his olive branch :—" Shure the best way to pacify Oireland is for the Queen to marry Parnell." A more practicable method than either is silently making headway against the elements of disorder; and in spite of the upsetters and their opposition the rough things will be made smooth, and the troubled waters will run clear, if only the Government of order may be allowed time to do its beneficent work of repression and re-establishment thoroughly and to the roots.

II.

IN politics, as in nature, beneficent powers work quietly, while destructive agencies sweep across the world with noise and tumult. The fruit tree grows in silence ; the tempest which uproots it shakes the earth to its centre. The gradual evolution of society in the development of art, the softening of manners, the equalization of justice, the respect for law, the purity of morals, which are its results and correlatives, comes about as silently as the growth of the tree ; but the wars which desolate nations, and the revolutions which destroy in a few months the work of many centuries, are as tumultuous as the tempest and as boisterous as the storm.

In Ireland at the present moment this rule holds good with surprising accuracy. Where the tranquilizing effect of Lord Ashbourne's Act attracts but little attention outside its own immediate sphere, the Plan of Campaign has everywhere been accompanied with murder, boycotting, outrage, and the loud cries of those who, playing at bowls, have to put up with rubbers. Where men who have retained their sense of manly honesty and commercial justice, buy their lands in peace, without asking the world to witness the transaction—those tenants who, having for years refused to pay a reduced rent or any portion of arrears, are at last evicted from the land they do not care to hold as honest men should, make the political welkin ring with their complaints, and call on the nation at large to avenge their wrongs. And the analogy holds good all through. The Irish tenant yearns to possess the land he farms. Lord Ashbourne's Act enables him to do this by the benign way of peace, fairness, and self-respect. The Plan of Campaign, on the other hand, teaches him the destructive methods of dishonesty and violence. The one is a legal, quiet, and equitable arrangement, without personal bitterness, without hysterical shrieking, without wrong-doing to any one. The other is an offence against the common interests of society, and a breach of the law accompanied by crimes against humanity. The one is silent and beneficent ; the other noisy, uprooting, and malevolent. But as the powers of growth and development are, in the long run, superior to those of destruction—else all would have gone by the board ages ago—the good done by Lord Ashbourne's Act will be a living force in the national history when the evil wrought by the Plan of Campaign is dead and done with.

By Lord Ashbourne's Act the Irish tenant can buy his farm at (an average of) seventeen years' purchase. He borrows the purchase money from the Government, paying it back on easy terms, so that in forty-nine years he becomes the absolute owner of the property— paying meantime in interest and gradual diminution of the principal, less than the present rent. The landlord has about £68 for every £100 he used to have in rent. This Act is quietly revolutionizing Ireland, redeeming it from agrarian anarchy, and saving the farmer from himself and his friends. Thousands and thousands of acres are being constantly sold in all parts of the country, and good prices are freely given for farms whereof the turbulent and discontented tenants professed themselves unable to pay the most moderate rents. Large holdings and small alike are bought as gladly as they are sold. Those who buy know the capabilities of the land when worked with a will; those who sell prefer a reduced certainty to the greater nominal value, which might vanish altogether under the fiat of the Campaigners and the visits of Captain Moonlight.

The Irish loyal papers, which no English Home Ruler ever sees—facts being so inimical to sentiment— these Irish papers are full of details respecting these sales. On one estate thirty-seven farmers buy their holdings at prices varying from £18 to £520, the average being £80. On another, six farms bring £5,603, one fetching £2,250. In the west, small farmers are buying where they can. In Sligo the MacDermott, Q.C., has sold farms to forty-two of his tenants for £3,096, the prices varying from £32 to £70 and £130; and the O'Connor Don has sold farms in the same county to fifteen tenants for £1,934. The number of acres purchased under this Act for the three years ending August, 1888, are a trifle over 293,556.

The Government valuation is £171,774,000. The net rent is £190,181 12s. 9d. The purchase-money is £3,350,933. The average number of years' purchase is 17·6.

Perhaps the most important of all these sales are those on the Egmont estate in the very heart of one of the gravely-disturbed districts. The rent-roll of this estate was £16,000 a year; and it was estimated that successive landlords had laid out about £250,000 in improvements—which was just the sum expected

to be realized by the sales. All this land has
passed into the hands of farmers who, from agitators
and No Renters have now become proprietors on their
own account, with a direct interest in maintaining law
and order, and in opposing violence and disorder all
round. Other important sales have been effected. A
hundred and fifty tenants on the Drapers' estate in
county Derry have bought their farms from the
London Company at a total of £57,980. These, with
others (197 in all), reached a sum total of purchase-
money of £63,305, as set forth in the *Dublin Gazette*, of
November 5th, 1889.

Lord Spencer, whose political *volte face* is one of
the wonders of the hour, does not hesitate to say
that this Act has not been a success. Can he give
counter figures to those quoted above? And Mr.
Michael Davitt does not approve of the sales in
general and of those on the Egmont estates in especial.
" He hates the Ashbourne Act worse than he hates the
idea of an endowed Roman Catholic University, which
is saying a great deal. He hates it because it renders
impossible his visionary scheme of land nationalization,
but more because it wrests from his hands the weapons
of Separatist rebellion. And what he openly says, all
the more cautious members of his party think. Every
purchaser under the Ashbourne Act is a soldier lost to
the cause of sedition. More than one of the ringleaders
have indeed said this formerly, but of late they have
grown more reticent. The Parnellite, it has been said,
is essentially an Opportunist. Mr. Davitt is hardly a
Parnellite, but the real Parnellite items have dis-
covered that their seats in Parliament and their

future hopes would be endangered, if they openly fell foul of the Act under which so many Irish tenants are becoming freeholders. They do not bless the Act, but they leave it alone."

There is another misstatement that had better be frankly met. The objectors to the Land Courts say that the applicants are so many and the process is so slow, it is almost useless and worse than heartbreaking to apply for relief. One thing, however, must be remembered—during the interim of application and hearing, a tenant cannot be disturbed in his holding, and if he refuses to pay his rent the landlord cannot evict him. The following correspondence is instructive :—

"Braintree, Nov. 14.

"Sir,—Will you be good enough to inform me whether the statement I give below is correct ? It was made by an Irish lecturer (going about with magic-lantern views) for the purpose of showing how unjustly the Irish tenants are treated. The lecturer was Mr. J. O'Brady, and he was delivering the lecture at Braintree on Saturday, November 9 :—' There are now 90,000 cases awaiting the decision of the Land Courts to fix a " fair rent " on their holdings, and as only 15,000 cases can be heard in one year, do you wonder at the tenants refusing to pay their present rent ? '

"Your faithful servant,

"G. THORPE BARTRAM."

"The Right Hon. A. J. Balfour, M.P."

" Irish Office, Great Queen Street, Nov. 22.

" Dear Sir,—I have made special inquiry into the subject of your letter of the 14th inst., and find that on the 31st of the last month the number of outstanding applications to have fair rents fixed was 44,295, and that the number of cases disposed of in the months of July and August (the latest month for which the figures are made up) was 5,380. You will see, therefore, that the arrear is less than one-half of the amount stated by the Separatist lecturer to whom you refer, and the rate of progression in disposing of it is considerably higher than that alleged by him. It may reasonably be hoped also (though the statistics are not yet available) that this rate has since been increased, as several additional Sub-Commissioners have been appointed to hear the cases. I would observe also that under the provisions of the Land Act, passed by the present Government in 1887, the tenant gets the benefit of the judicial rent from the date of his application, an advantage which he did not possess under Mr. Gladstone's Act. Such unavoidable delay as may occur, therefore, does not, under the existing law, involve the serious injury to the tenant implied by the lecturer. I enclose a printed paper, which will give you further information on this subject. In conclusion, I would point out that the suggestion that the agrarian trouble in Ireland arises from the difficulty experienced by the tenants in getting judicial rents fixed is not warranted by the facts. Take as illustrations the cases of two estates which have lately been prominently before the public—namely, the Ponsonby and the Olphert. In the former case the landlord is anxious, I believe, to get the tenants to go into Court, and offers to give retrospective effect to the decisions, though not bound by law to do so, but under the influence of the agitators the tenants refuse to go into Court. In the latter instance judicial rents have long since been fixed in the great majority of cases.

" Yours faithfully,

" Arthur James Balfour."

Together with this easy mode of purchase by which the quiet and industrious are profiting, rents are reduced all over the country, though still the Home Rulers reiterate the old charge of " rack-renting," as if such a thing were the rule. These unscrupulous misstatements, indeed, make half the difficulties of the Irish question ; for lies stick fast, where disclaimers, proofs, facts, and figures, pass by like dry leaves on the wind. But for all the fact of past extortion the present reductions are not always a proof of over-renting. What Mr. Buxton says has common sense on the face of it :—

" Very serious reductions of rents are being made all through Ireland by the Land Sub-Commissioners, who are supposed to be in some extent guided by the appearance of the farms. Now it should be remembered that at the interview that took place in London on July 3rd, between Mr. Smith-Barry and some of his tenants, in reference to that gentleman's support of the evictions on the Ponsonby estate, one of the arguments for forgiveness of arrears was that when eviction was threatened ' the tenants gave up their industry,' and ' how could they get the rents out of the land when they were absolutely idle ? ' To admit such a plea for granting a reduction of rent is most dangerous. Tenants

have but to neglect their land, get into arrears of rent,
and claim large reductions because their farms do not
pay. An ignorant, or slovenly, or idle farmer, under
such circumstances, is likely to have a lower rent fixed
by the Sub-Commissioners than his more industrious
neighbour, and thus a great injustice may be done to
both the good farmer and the landlord, the—perhaps
cunningly — idle farmer receiving a premium for
neglecting his farm. A comparison of the judicial
rents with the former rents and the Poor Law valuation is truly startling, and must lead one to imagine
that the system by which so much valuable property is
dealt with is most unjust."

Thus, the famous reductions in County Clare, where
the abatements granted averaged over 30 per cent.,
and in some cases exceeded 50 per cent., were not
perhaps all a sign of the landlord's iniquity, but also
may be taken to show something of the tenant's
indifference. Poverty is pitiable, truly, and it claims
relief from all who believe in the interdependence of a
community; but poverty which comes from idleness,
unthrift, neglect, and which then falls on others to
relieve—these others having to suffer for sins not their
own—how about that as a righteous obligation? Must
I and my children go foodless because my tenants will
neither till the land they hold from me, so as to make
it yield their own livelihood and that profit over which
is my inheritance, nor suffer others to do what they
will not? If we are prepared to endorse the famous
saying: " La propriété c'est le vol," well and good.
Meanwhile to spend all our sympathy on men who
reduce themselves and others to poverty by idleness

and unthrift, seems rather a bad investment of emotion. The old-fashioned saying about workers and eaters had a different ring; and once on a time birds who could sing, and would not, were somehow made.

Co-incident with these conditions of no rent at all—reduction of rent all round—and the free purchase of land by those who yesterday professed pauperism, is the startling fact that the increase in Bank deposits for the half-year of 1889 was £89,000—in Post Office Savings Bank deposits £244,000—in Trustee Savings Banks, £16,000.

Mr. Mitchell Henry, writing to the *Times*, says:— " If any one will tell the exact truth as to Irish matters at this moment, he must confess that landlords are utterly powerless to coerce their tenants; that the pockets of the tenants themselves are full of money formerly paid in rent; that the price of all kinds of cattle has risen largely; that the last harvest was an excellent one; and that the banks—savings banks, Post Office banks, and ordinary banks—are richer than they have ever been, whilst the consumption of whisky —that sure barometer of Irish prosperity—is increasing beyond all former experience. In addition to this, I venture to say that, with certain local exceptions, the Irish peasant is better clothed than any other peasants in the world. The people are sick of agitation and long to be let alone; but they are a people of extraordinary clannishness, and take an intellectual delight in intrigue, especially where the Saxon is concerned. British simplicity is wonderful, and the very people who have put on this cupboard love for Mr. Gladstone and his lieutenants, whom they formerly abused beyond all decent license of abuse, laugh at them as soon as their backs are turned."

These savings do not come from the landlords, so many of whom are hopelessly ruined by the combined action of our own legislature and the Plan of Campaign. Of this ruin Colonel Lloyd has given a very graphic account. Alluding to Mr. Balfour's answer in the House on the 21st of June, to the question put by Mr. Macartney on Colonel Lloyd's letter to the *Times* (10th of June), the Colonel repeats his assertions, or rather his accusations against the Court. These are :—" First, that the percentage of reductions now being given is the very highest yet made, notwithstanding that prices of agricultural produce and cattle have considerably increased ; secondly, that the Sub-Commissioners have no fixed rule to guide them save one—viz., that existing rents, be they high or low, must be cut down, although they may not have been altered for half a century; thirdly, that it was reported the Commissioners had instructions to give all-round reductions of 33 per cent. ; fourthly, that in the Land Court the most skilled evidence of value is disregarded, as also the Poor Law valuation ; fifthly, that the Sub-Commissioners assign no reasons for their decisions ; and, sixthly, that the machinery of the Court is faulty and unfair in the following instances :—(*a*) If a landlord appeals and fails, he must pay costs, but if he appeals and succeeds he will not get costs ; (*b*) tenants' costs are taxed by the Court behind the landlord's back ; (*c*) their rules are constantly changing without any proper notice to the public ; and (*d*) appeals are accumulating with no prospect of their being disposed of in any reasonable time."

Colonel Lloyd disposes of Mr. Balfour's denials to these statements, but at too great length to copy. It may be taken for granted here that they are disposed of, and that he proves up to the hilt his case of crying injustice to the landlords—as indeed every fair-minded person who looks honestly into the question, must acknowledge. As one slight corroboration of what he says he adduces the following instances :—

" The following judicial rents were fixed by the Assistant-Commissioners in the West of Ireland :—

Tenants' Names.				Old Rent.			Poor Law Valuation.			Judicial Rent.		
				£	s.	d.	£	s.	d.	£	s.	d.
Tom Regan	..	..	..	9	9	10	12	0	0	5	15	0
J. Manlon ..	..	..	..	9	2	6	11	10	0	5	15	0
C. Kelly ..	..	..	..	9	12	10	11	5	0	6	0	0
J. Kenny ..	..	..	..	4	11	4	6	5	0	2	15	0
				£32	16	6	£41	0	0	£20	5	0

" The landlord appealed, and the appeals were heard a few days ago by the Chief Commissioners in Roscommon. Two skilled valuers were employed, who valued within a few shillings of the Government valuation, and in the face of this evidence the decisions of the Assistant-Commissioners were confirmed. These are not by any means isolated instances. In fact they are the rule in the Land Court."

And he ends by this remarkable assertion :—

" The whole machinery of the Court must be remodelled if it is to possess the confidence of the public. As it is at present composed, it is too much subject to political influence and to the clamour of one set of litigants to be independent. There are few of your readers, I

believe, who will not admit that it is a very alarming
thing to find a Court so constituted having the control
of millions. The only officials ever connected with the
Court in which there was any degree of confidence were
the Court valuers attached to the Appeal Court. They
were men of independence and impartiality, but they
were dispensed with in a vain attempt to satisfy Mr.
Parnell. I see by Mr. Balfour's statement in the
House of Commons on the 25th ult. that the Chief
Commissioners are again engaged in framing new rules
with regard to appeals. One would think that at the
end of eight years they would have had their rules
complete, and that an alteration every three months
during that period ought to have brought them to
perfection. How long is this farce to continue? These
are serious complaints against a public body intrusted
with the administration of justice. They do not
deserve to be lightly passed over, and I am confident
that, even should it suit the convenience of the present
Government to follow the example of their predecessors
and ignore them, the English people, with their strong
sense of justice, will eventually insist on the unfair
treatment and glaring injustice and abuses complained
of being set right, and that those who have from political
motives and influence been placed in honourable and
responsible judicial positions shall give place to
impartial men, who will deal out even-handed justice
to the landlord as well as to the tenant.—I remain your
obedient servant,

" JESSE LLOYD, Lieutenant-Colonel and J.P.,
" Agent for Lord Rossmore.
" Rossmore Agency Office, Monaghan."

Here, then, is the reverse of the medal. Hitherto the outcry has been all for the tenant, and I do not say for a moment that this outcry was not just. It was. The Irish peasant has had his wrongs, deep and shameful ; but now justice has been done to him so amply that the overflow has gone to the other side. It is time to look at things as they are, and to let well alone. Justice to the one has broadened out into persecution of the other, and an Irish landlord is for the moment the favourite cock-shy for aggressive legislation. But, as I have said before, prejudice dies hard, and sentimental pity is often only prejudice in a satin cloak. The Irish peasant is still assumed to be a helpless victim, the Irish landlord a ruffianly tyrant ; and a state of things as obsolete as the Ogham language itself still rouses active passion as against a living wrong. I go back to that statement in the *Pall Mall Gazette*, to which I have before alluded, as an instance of the way in which the very froth of prejudice and falsehood is whipped up into active poison by the short and easy way of imagination and assertion. It is a fair sample of all the rest ; but these are the things which find credit with those who do not know and do not enquire.

Advocating the making of blackberry wine as the short cut from poverty to prosperity in Ireland, the scheme being parallel to Mr. Gladstone's famous remedy of jam, this sapient " B.O'N." says :—

" The blackberry harvest would be over in the sunny Rhine country before it began in Ireland. Why should not some practical natives go over from home and see how it is all done ? I quite know that any plan for

bettering the physical condition of our people is open
to the objection that as soon as they seem a little ' com-
fortable' the landlord would raise the rent in many a
case; but perhaps in a still larger number of cases he
would now be afraid to do so. And I know, too, that
even a blackberry wine industry will not be quite safe
till we have Home Rule; but is not that coming
fast ? "

This mischievous little word is in the very teeth of
the fact that rents cannot be raised on any plea what-
soever—certainly not because the tenant makes himself
better off by an industry other than his farming—and
that the whole machinery of Government had been put
in motion to protect the land tiller from the land-
owner. Yet the *Pall Mall Gazette* is not ashamed to
lend itself to this lie on the chance of catching a few
fluttering minds and nailing them to the mast of Home
Rule on the false supposition that this means justice to
the oppressed tenant and wholesome restraint of the
brutal proprietor. Professor Mahaffy, in a long letter
to the *New York Independent*, speaks of the same kind of
thing still going on in America—this bolstering up a
delusion by statements as far removed from the truth
as that of " B.O'N.'s," to which the *Pall Mall Gazette*
gives sanction and circulation. That part of the
American press which is under the influence or control
of the Irish Home Rulers still goes on talking of the
oppression to which the Irish tenant is subjected, just
as the speeches of the Agitators (*vide* the astounding
lies, as well as the appalling nonsense talked, when
Lady Sandhurst and Mr. Stansfeld were made citizens
of Dublin, and it was asserted that the Government

turned tail and fled before these "delegates") teem
with analogous assertions wherein not so much as one
grain of truth is to be found. Let it be again repeated
in answer to all these falsehoods :—No tenant can be
evicted except for non-payment of one year's rent ; that
rent can be settled by the courts, and if he has signed
an agreement for an excessive payment, his agreement
can be broken ; and he must be compensated for all the
improvements he has made or will swear that he has
made. Also, he can borrow money from the Government at the lowest possible interest, and become the
owner of his farm for less yearly payment than his
former rent. He, the Irish tenant, is the most protected,
the most favoured of all leaseholders in Europe or
America, but the old cries are raised, the old watch-
words are repeated, just as if nothing had been done
since the days when he was as badly off as the Egyptian
fellah, and was, in truth, between the devil and the
deep sea. Let me repeat the legal and actual
condition of things as summarized by Mr. Montagu
Crackanthorpe, Q.C. These six propositions ought to
be learned by heart before anyone allows himself to
talk of Home Rule or the Irish question :—

1. That every yearly tenant of agricultural land
valued at less than £50 a year can have his rent
judicially fixed, and that the existence of arrears of rent
creates no statutory obstacle whatever, nor any
difficulty in procedure, if he is desirous of availing
himself of the Acts.

2. That every such agricultural tenant, whether he
has had a fair rent fixed or not, may sell his tenancy
to the highest bidder whenever he desires to leave ;

and that, if he be evicted, he has the right either to
redeem within six months, or to sell his tenancy
within the same period to a purchaser, who can likewise redeem, and thus acquire all the privileges of the
tenant.

3. That in view of the fall in agricultural produce,
the Land Commission is empowered and directed to
vary the rents fixed by the Land Court during the
years 1881 to 1885, in accordance with the difference
in prices of produce between those years and the years
1887 to 1889.

4. That no tenant in Ireland can be evicted by his
landlord unless his rent is twelve months in arrear, and
that the yearly tenant who is so evicted must be paid
full compensation for all improvements not already
compensated for by enjoyment, such, for instance, as
unexhausted manure, permanent buildings, and reclamation of waste land. He may, it is true, be evicted on
title after judgment obtained against him for his rent,
and in that case his goods and interest (including his
improvements) may be put up to auction by the Sheriff.
This is a matter which seems to require amendment;
but it is to be observed that the same consequences
would follow if the judgment creditor were a shop-
keeper who had given the tenant credit or the local
money-lender or gombeen man. A compulsory sale
under these circumstances is not peculiar to landlordism, and it is a method to which landlords seldom
resort.

5. That if a tenant falls into arrear for rent, and
becomes liable to eviction, whether on title or not, the
Court can stay process, if satisfied that his difficulty

arises from no fault of his own, and can give him time to pay by instalments.

6. That if a tenant wishes to buy his holding, and comes to terms with his landlord, he can borrow money from the Government at 4 per cent., by the help of which he may change his rent into an annuity, the amount of the annuity being less than the rent, and the burden of the annuity altogether ceasing at the end of forty-nine years.

The result by the way of this peasant proprietorship will be twofold. On the one side it will create a greater uniformity of comfort and a larger class of peaceable, self-respecting, law-abiding citizens. On the other it will lower the general standard by doing away with that better class of resident gentry and capitalized landowners, who in their way are guides, teachers and helps to the peasantry. The absence of this better class of resident gentry is one of the misfortunes of French agricultural life and the justification of M. Zola ; their presence is one of the blessings of England. How will it be in Ireland when the exodus is more complete than it is even now, and when the villages and rural districts are left solely to peasant proprietors and a celibate clergy ? The Romish Church has never been famous for teaching those things which make for intellectual enlightenment and social improvement. The difference between the Protestant north and the rest of Roman Catholic Ireland, as between the Protestant and Romish cantons in Switzerland ; is a truism almost proverbial. And without the little leaven of such influence as the better educated and more enlightened gentry may possess, the Irish peasant will be even more super-

stitious, more blinded by prejudice and ignorance than
he is now. As it is, the old landlords are sincerely
deplored, and the good they did is as sincerely regretted.
Those grand old hunting days, now things of the past,
still linger in the memory of the men who participated
in the fun and had their full share of the crumbs—
and the times when a grand seigneur paid a hundred
pounds à week in wages alone seem something like
glimpses into a railed and fenced off El Dorado, which
the Plan of Campaign has closed for ever. So that the
sunshine has its shadow, for all the good to be had from
the light.

It ought to be that peasant proprietorship will make
the holder more industrious and a better farmer than
he has been as tenant. Whether it will or not remains
to be seen. As things are—always excepting Ulster
and the North generally—farming could scarcely be
more shameful in its neglect than it is—domestic life
could scarcely be more squalid, more savage, more filthy.
Even rich farmers live like pigs and with their pigs, and
the stone house is no better kept than the mud cabin—
the forty-acre field no better tilled than the miserable
little potato patch. Had the farming been better, there
would never have been the poverty, the discontent, the
agitation by which Ireland had been tortured and con-
vulsed. Had the men been more industrious, the
women cleaner and more deft, the Plan of Campaign
would have failed for want of social nutriment, where
now it has been so disastrously triumphant. Physical
well-being is a great incentive to quiet living—produc-
tive industry checks political unrest. Those who have
something to lose are careful to keep it ; and we may

be sure that Captain Moonlight would not risk his skin if he had a good coat to cover it.

Also there is another aspect in which this land question may be viewed, and ought to be viewed—in reference to the manner in which the Irish farmer treats the property by which he lives :—that is the aspect of his duty to the community in his quality of producer for the community. We must all come down to the land as the common property of the human race. Parcelled out as it may be —by the mile or the square yard—it is the common mother of all men. We can do without everything else, from lace to marble—from statues to carriages—but food we must have ; and the holders of land all the world over are really and rightfully trustees for the race. The Irish peasant has no more right to neglect the possibilities of produce than had William Rufus, or his modern representative in Scotland, to evict villages for the making of a deer forest. The principle of trusteeship in the land holds good with small holders and great alike ; but imagine what would be the effect of a law which required so much produce from a given area on an average for so long a period ! The principle is of course conceded in the rent, rates and taxes ; but a direct application to produce would set the kingdom in a blaze.

But in Ireland fields of thistles and acres of ragwort, with tall purple spikes of loose strife everywhere, seem to be held as valid crops, fit for food and good at rent-paying. These are to be found at every step from Dublin to Kerry, and the most unpractised eye can see the waste and neglect and unnecessary squalor of both

land and people. As an English farmer said, with
indignation : "The land is brutally treated." So it is—
idleness, unthrift, and bad farming generally, degrading
it far below its possibilities and natural standard of production. Cross the Channel, and Wales looks like a trim
garden. Go over to France, and you find every yard of
soil carefully tilled and cultivated. Even in comparatively
ramshackle Sicily, among the old lava beds of Etna,
the peasants raise a handful of grain on the top of a
rock no bigger than a lady's work-table. In Ireland
the cultivated portion of a holding is often no bigger
relatively than that work-table on an acre of waste.
Will the tiller, now the owner and no longer only the
leaseholder, go back from his evil ways of thriftlessness
and neglect, and instead of being content to live just
above the line of starvation, will he educate himself up
to those artificial wants which only industry can supply ?
Will the women learn to love cleanliness, to regard
their men's rags and their children's dirt as their own
dishonour, and to understand that womanhood has its
share of duties in social and domestic life ? Will the
sense of beauty grow with the sense of proprietorship,
and the filth of the present surroundings be replaced
by a flower garden before the cottage—a creeper against
the wall—a few pots of more delicate blooms in the
window ? Will the taste for variety in garden produce be enlarged, and plots of peas, beans, carrots,
artichokes, pot-herbs, and the like, be added to the one
monotonous potato-patch, with a few cabbages and
roots for the baste, and a strip of oats as the sole cereal
attempted ? Who knows ? At present there is not a
flower to be seen in the whole of the West, save those

which a luxuriant Nature herself has sown and planted ;
and the immediate surroundings of the substantial
farm-house, like those of the mud cabin, are filth unmen-
tionable, savage squalor, and bestial neglect.

These things are signs of a mental and moral condition that goes deeper than the manifestation. They do
not show only want of the sense of beauty—want of
the sense even of cleanliness; they show the absence
of all the civilizing influences—all the humanizing
tendencies of modern society. By this want Ireland is
made miserable and kept low in the scale of nations.
Had the race been self-respecting, sturdy, upright,
stubbornly industrious, all this savage neglect would
have mended itself. Being what it is—excitable,
imaginative, spasmodic, given over to ideas rather
than to facts, and trusting to Hercules in the clouds
rather than to its own brawny shoulders—this squalor
continues and is not dependent on poverty. Time alone
will show whether changed agrarian conditions will
alter it. So far as his power goes, the priest does
nothing to touch it. The Church uses up its influence
for everything but the practical purposes of work-a-day-
life. It teaches obediences to its ordinances, but not
civic virtues. It encourages boys and girls to marry at
an age when they neither understand the respon-
sibilities of life nor can support a family ; but in its
regard for the Sacrament it forgets the pauperization
of the nation. It enforces chastity, but it winks at
murder; it demands money for masses for the souls of
the dead, but it leaves on one side the homes and
bodies of the living ; it breeds a race of paupers to drag
the country lower and lower into the depths of poverty,

and thinks it has done a meritorious work, and one that calls for praise because of the paucity of numbers in the percentage of illegitimate births. Thus in Ireland, where everything is set askew, even morality has its drawbacks, and less individual virtue would be a distinct national gain.

The Home Rule enthusiasts say all that is wanted to remedy these ingrained defects is a Parliament ; all that is wanted to make Irishmen perfect and Ireland a paradise is a Parliament chosen by the people and sitting in College Green. Human nature will then be changed, and the lion and the lamb will lie down together. The Papist will love the Protestant, and the moral of the story about those two Scotch Presbyterian boys, whose presence at the Barrow House National School so seriously disturbed both priest and people, is one that will read quite the other way. All the bitter hatred poured out against England, against Protestants, against the law and its administrators, will cease so soon as Catholics come to the place of power and the supremacy of England is at an end. The Church which burned Giordano Bruno and is affronted because his memory has been honoured—which placed the Quirinale under the ban of the lesser excommunication, and withstood the national impulse towards freedom and unity as represented by Garibaldi—the Church which has ever been on the side of intolerance and tyranny will suddenly, in Ireland under Home Rule, become beneficent, just, and liberal, and heretics will no longer herd with the goats but will take their place among the sheep. If, as Mr. Redmond says, it is the duty of Irishmen to make the Government of England an impossibility, it will then be their pleasure to make her alliance both close and easy. Ulster and Kerry will march shoulder to shoulder, and Leaguers and Orangemen will form an unbroken phalanx of orderly and law-abiding citizens. In a word the old Dragon will be chained and the Millenium will come.

The prospect seems too good to be true. Were we to follow after it and put the loyal Protestant minority into the power of the anti-imperial Catholic majority in the hope of seeking peace and ensuing it, we might perchance be like the dog who let fall that piece of meat from between his teeth—losing the substance for shadow. We do better, all things considered, with our present arrangements—trusting to the imperfect operations of human law rather than shooting Niagara for the chance of the clear stream at the bottom.

The whirligig of Time has changed the relative positions of the two great parties in Ireland. Formerly it was the Catholics who desired the abolition of Home Rule, and the Protestants who held by the National Parliament. That Parliament was exclusively Protestant, and the powerful minority ground the helpless majority to the very ground. Catholics were persecuted from shore to shore, and all sorts and conditions of Protestant bullies and tyrants sent up petitions to forbid the iniquity of Catholic trade rivalry. What was then would be now—changing the venue and putting the Catholics where the Protestants used to be. We do not believe that the " principle of Nationality " is the working power of this desire for Home Rule, as Mr. Stansfeld asserts—unless indeed the principle of Nationality can be stretched so as to cover the self-aggrandizement of a party, the bitterness of religious hatred, and the tyranny of a cruel and coercive combination. The grand and noble name of Nationality can scarcely be made so elastic as this. Respect for law lies at the very heart of the principle, and the Irish Home Rulers are of all men the most conspicuous for their contempt of law and their bold infraction of the very elementary ordinances of civilized society.

As for tyranny, no coercion established by Government—not even that proclaimed by Mr. Gladstone—has been more stringent than the coercion exercised by the Plan of Campaign. What happened in Tipperary only the other day when certain rent-paying tenants, who had been boycotted, did public penance in the following propositions? They offered:—" Firstly, to come forward to the subsequent public meeting and express public contrition for having violated their resolution to hold out with the other tenants ; secondly, not to pay the next half-year's rent, due on the 10th of December, but to in future act with the general body of the tenantry: and thirdly, to pay each a pecuniary sum, to be halved between the Ponsonby tenants and the Smith-Barry Tipperary tenantry in the fight which is to come on." Surely no humiliation was ever greater than this!—no decree of secret council or pitiless Vehmgericht were ever more ruthlessly imposed, more servilely obeyed ! Can we say that the Irish are fit to be called freemen, or able to exercise the real functions of Nationality, when they can suffer themselves to be hounded like sheep and rated like dogs for the exercise of their own judgment and the performance of their duties as honest men and good citizens ?

If the mere presence in Ireland of Lady Sandhurst
and Mr. Stansfeld dismayed Mr. Balfour and scattered
his myrmidons as the forces of the Evil One fly before
the advent of the angels, could they not have used their
semi-divine power for these humiliated rent-payers?
Instead of complacently listening to bunkum—which, if
they had had any sense of humour would have made
them laugh; any of modesty would have made them
blush—could they not have brought their inherited
principles of commercial honesty and manly fidelity to
an engagement to bear on these irate Campaigners,
and have reminded them that the very core of Liberalism
is the right of each man to unrestricted action, provided
he does not hurt his neighbour? But Home Rulers are
essentially one-sided in their estimate of tyranny, and
things change their names according to the side on
which they are ranged. To boycott a man, to mutilate
his cattle,* to commit outrages on his family, and finally
to murder him outright for paying his rent or taking
an evicted farm, are all justifiable proceedings of
righteous severity. But for a landlord to evict a
tenant from the farm for which he will not pay the
covenanted rent—will not, but yet could, twice over—
is a cowardly, a brutal, a damnable act, for which those
slugs from behind a stone-wall are the well-deserved
reward.

Here is an instance of the vengeance sought to

---

* The Irish have always been cruel to animals. It is a curious
fact that most Roman Catholic peasants are. In the time of
Charles I. an Act was passed to prevent the Irish farmers from
ploughing by their oxens' tails. Even now they pluck their
geese alive.

be taken by wealthy tenants evicted for non-payment of rent.

" Lord Clanricarde writes to the *Times* to corroborate the statement that an infernal explosive machine had been found in a cottage at Woodford, in Ireland. His lordship quotes as follows from the account of an eye-witness :—

' When possession was taken of the sub-tenant's house, No. 1, there was the usual crowd crowding as close to our party as the police would allow ; but it was remarked that on our approach to houses Nos. 2 and 3, close together, and which concealed the infernal machine, the crowd kept well away out of hearing, while the Woodford leaders were on a car on the road, but out of danger like the others ; but all well in sight of any destruction that might befall the officers of the law. This house, No. 3, when last examined in June, was found vacant, door not locked, but open, and used as a shelter for cattle. Finding it locked now, X. detached the lock, pushed the door open, and he and I and others went inside. The house was empty, but a pile of stones was heaped up in the doorway, some of them had been displaced by the door when opened, and the top of a box 6 in. square was seen embedded in a barrel containing 25 lbs. of ' excellent gunpowder,' a bottle full of sulphuric acid, and other explosives, as well as a number of denotators, and the blade of a knife (apparently) with a spring attached by a coil of string to the door, the machine being so arranged as to be liable to explode in two ways. The expert who examined the machine said that had the sulphuric acid been liberated, as meant, all our party, twenty in all,

must have been destroyed, as there were enough
explosives to destroy any living thing within 100 yards.
Neither on that day, nor on the 22nd (date of sale)
did either the tenant or the Woodford leaders—
R. and K.—utter one word of surprise, much less of
abhorrence ! '

The tenant proceeded against (says Lord Clanricarde,
owed four and a-half years' rent, at £47 8s. per annum)
much below the taxation valuation of £67 19s., for a
mill, with the sole use of the water-power, a valuable
privilege, and 440 statute acres, a considerable part of
them arable land. He had ten sub-tenants, was
reported to make £500 per annum from mill and farm,
and though he had removed part of his stock, there
were still cattle on the land on the day of eviction
enough to cover two years' arrears. If he had paid
even those two years on account he would have
received an abatement, and saved his farm. The
judge in Dublin who gave the decree against him,
gave also costs against him to mark his sense of the
tenant's bad conduct."

And to think that good, honest, noble-hearted, and
sincere Englishmen, who in their own persons are law-
abiding, just, honourable, and faithful, should uphold a
state of things which strikes at the root of all law, all
commercial honesty—blinded as they are by the glamour
of a generous, unreal, and unworkable sentiment ! If
only they would go over to Ireland to judge for themselves on the basis of facts, not fancies—and to be
informed by truths not lies !

I know that we cannot all see alike, and that every
shield has its two sides. In this matter, on the one

side stand Earl Spencer, now converted to Home Rule,
since his Viceroyalty; on the other is the example of
Mr. Forster, who went to Ireland an ardent Home
Ruler and came back as strong a Unionist. The
Quaker became a fighting man, and the idealist a
practical man, believing in facts as he had seen them
and no longer in sentiments he could not realise—in
measures grounded on the necessities of good government, and not like so many epiphytes with their roots in
the air. Let Lord Spencer bring to this test his late
utterances. He goes in now for Home Rule, and the
right of Ireland to appoint her own police and judges.
He is out of the wood and can hallo; but where would
he have been if the Irish had appointed their police
when he was at the Castle ?—with Lord Frederick and
Mr. Burke ! And if the judges were appointed by the
Irish, we should have, in all probability, Mr. Tim
Harrington, barrister-at-law, on the bench; and a few
years ago Mr. Tim Harrington crumpled up the Queen's
writ and flung it out of the Court House window. And
what power over the fortunes of others can be given to
men who boycott a railway for political spite ? *

---

* The boycott against the Great Northern Railway line between
Carrickmacross and Dundalk is now in full swing. It was begun at
Friday's fair in the former town, intimation having been given to
all dealers in cattle and pigs that not an animal was to leave by the
Great Northern line. Not a hackney car was permitted to attend
the railway station, and commercial travellers had to leave their
samples at the station. Many of the cattle and pigs purchased at
the fair were driven by road to Kingscourt, where there is a station
of the Midland Great Western Company, a local National League
branch having published a resolution recommending all goods to be
sent and received *via* Kingscourt. It has also been resolved to do

So many things have conspired to make this Irish question a Gordian-knot which no man can untie, and but few would dare to cut. The past extravagance of the landlords, absenteeism, rack-renting, injustice of all kinds ; the past jealousy of England and her over-shadowing all native industries and productions ; difference of religion, racial temperament, and the irreconcilable enmity of the conquered towards the conquerors ; ignorance and idleness ; the morality which marries too early, when the land, which was just enough to support one family, is expected to keep three or four ; want of self-respect in the dirt and

---

no business with commercial travellers from Belfast, or other parts of the North of Ireland, whose goods had been carried over the Great Northern system. Travellers from Scotland, England, and Dublin are only to be dealt with under guarantees that they do not use the Great Northern line.

BOYCOTTING IN COUNTY WATERFORD.

THE LEAGUE'S BLACK LIST.

There has been issued by the National League in the county Waterford a " list of objectionable persons, with whom it is expected that no true man will have any dealings whatever "—cattle dealers, butter merchants, grain and hay merchants, brokers, and farmers being specially enjoined to refrain from any dealings with them, the farmers being told that they " must carefully avoid " the sale of milk or stock to agents of objectionable persons, and evicted tenants that they " must deem it their strict and imperative duty to follow to the markets all stock and produce reared upon their farms."

Look, too, at the abuse poured out on all the Government leaders and officials. In the *Freeman's Journal*, of December 5th, is one of the most disgraceful attacks on Mr. Balfour ever made by journalism. It reads like a filthy outpour of a Yahoo rather than the utterance of a sane and responsible man. Are these the minds to govern a great and honest country ?

disorder of domestic life; want of all communal life
or amusement, save in heated politics and drink; bogs
here, unthrift there, small holdings everywhere—all
these things help to complicate a question which
passion has already made too difficult for even the
most radical kind of statesmanship to adjust. All the
panaceas hitherto tried have been found ineffectual.
The repeal of Catholic disabilities, the establishment
of national schools, the disestablishment of the Protestant Church, the Maynooth grant, the various Land
Acts—all have done but little towards the settlement of
the question, which, like certain fabulous creatures,
has increased in strength and the extensions of its
demands by every concession made. The best
chance yet offered seems to be in the quiet working
of Lord Ashbourne's Act, by which the tenant becomes
the owner and the landlord is not despoiled. And
certainly the crying need of the moment is legislative
finality and political rest. Existing machinery is
sufficient for all the agrarian ameliorations demanded.
To do much more would be to act like children who
pluck up their seeds to see how they are growing,
leaving nothing sufficient time for development or
reproduction.

No one would deny such a measure of Home Rule
to Ireland as should give her the management of her
own internal affairs, in the same manner and degree as
our County Councils are to manage ours. But this is
not the Home Rule demanded by the leaders of the
party. That for which they have taken off their coats
means the loss of the country as an integral part of the
Empire; the oppression and practical annihilation of

the Protestant section ; the opening of the Irish ports
to all the enemies of England ; or the breaking out of
civil war in Ireland and its reconquest by England.
The alternative scheme of federation is for the moment
unworkable. But to hand over the whole conduct of
Irish affairs to the Roman Catholic majority would be
one of those ineffaceable political crimes the greatness
of which would be equalled only by the magnitude of
its mistake. The language of the indigenous Home
Rulers and their Transatlantic sympathisers—as well
as the things they have done and are still doing—ought
to be warnings sufficiently strong to prevent such an
act of folly and wickedness on our part. Even our men—
men of light and leading like Mr. John Morley—seem
to lose their heads when they approach the Irish
question and to become as rabid in their accusations as
the paid political agitators themselves. I will give these
two short extracts, the one from Mr. Morley's speech
at Glasgow, and the other from Lord Powerscourt's
temperate and rational commentary :—

" Mr. Morley says," quotes Lord Powerscourt, " that
the Irish people are more backward than the Scotch
or English, which I venture to doubt, at least as regards
intelligence, and gives as the reason :—

" ' It is because the landlords, who have been their
masters, have rack-rented them, have sunk them in
poverty, have plundered their own improvements, have
confiscated the fruits of their own industry, have done
all that they could to degrade their manhood. That
is why they are backward. (Cheers.) Will anybody
deny that the Irish landlords are open to this great
accusation and indictment ? If anybody here is inclined

to deny it, let him look at the reductions in rent that
have been made since 1881 in the Land Court.'

" Well, have not rents in England and Scotland
been reduced quite as much, nay, more, than Irish
rents since 1881 ? And have not the economic causes
which have lowered the prices of all farm produce all
over Europe caused the same depreciation in the value
of land in Germany or France, for instance, in the
same ratio as in Ireland ? And has not the importa-
tion of dead meat from America, Australia, or New
Zealand had something to do with it ?

" These facts are well known. But to return to the
Irish landlords. Does not every one who is resident in
Ireland, and therefore conversant with the state of
affairs there for the last twenty or thirty years, know
that the discontent and uprising against the land system
is due to the action of a very few unjust persons, now
mostly dead, but whose names are well known to any
one who really knows Ireland, as I venture to maintain Mr. Morley does not ? The principal actors in
the drama could be counted on the fingers of one hand.
And Mr. Morley, *ex uno disce omnes*, accuses the whole of
the Irish proprietors of these cruel and unjust practices
which we should scorn to be guilty of. And he is an ex-
Cabinet Minister, and late Chief Secretary for Ireland
for a few months, and a very popular one he was !

" He says, again : ' Public opinion would have
checked the Irish landlords in their infatuated policy
towards their tenants,' &c. He challenges denial of
these charges. Well, I deny them most emphatically,
and am quite willing to abide by the verdict of the
respectable tenants. I throw back in his face the

accusation that the Irish landlords as a body have rack-rented or plundered their tenants or confiscated their improvements.

" Far be it from me to taunt the Irish population. No, they have been tempted very sorely by prospects being held out to them of getting the land for nothing, and, all things considered, it is wonderful how they have behaved. But Mr. Morley is like many another politician who comes to Ireland for a few months or a few weeks, and goes about the few disturbed districts and listens to all the tales told him by cardrivers and those very clever people who delight in gulling the Saxon, and goes back to England, full of all sorts of horrors and crimes alleged to have been perpetrated by landlords, and takes it all as gospel, making no allowance for the great intelligence and inventive genius of his informers, and says, ' Oh ! I went to the place, and saw it all.' And this he takes to represent the normal state of the whole of Ireland, and makes it a justification of the Plan of Campaign ! "

Take too the Irish Home Rule press, and read the floods of abuse—some spreading out into absolute obscenity—published by the principal papers day after day against all their political opponents, and we can judge of the temper with which the Irish Home Rulers would administer affairs. Of their statesmanlike provision—of their patriotism and care for the well-being of the country at large—the local war now ruining Tipperary is the negative proof—the damnatory evidence that they are utterly unfit for practical power. Governed by hysterical passion, by mad hatred and the desire for revenge, not one of the modern leaders, save Mr.

Parnell, shows the faintest trace of politic self-control or the just estimate of proportions. To spite their opponents they will ruin themselves and their friends, as they have done scores of times, and are doing now in Tipperary. History holds up its hands in horror at the French Terror—was that worse than the system of murder and boycotting and outrage and terrorism in the disturbed districts in Ireland? And would it be a right thing for England to give the supreme power to these masked Couthons and Robespierres and Marats, that they might extend their operations into the now peaceable north, and reproduce in Ulster the tragedies of the south and west? Mr. Parnell puts aside the tyrannous part of the business, and cleverly throws the whole weight of his argument at Nottingham into the passionless economic scales. All that the Nationalist party desires, he says, " is to be allowed to develope the resources of their own country at their own expense," "without any harm to you (English), without any diminution of your resources, without any risk to your credit, or call upon you," all to be done "at our own expense and out of our own resources." Yet Mr. Parnell in another breath describes Ireland as " a Lazarus by the wayside "—a country " where unfortunately there is no manufacturing industry." " Ex nihilo nihil fit," was a lesson we all learned in our school days. Mr. Parnell has evidently forgotten his.

I will give a commentary on these brave words which is better put than I could put it.

To the Editor of the " Standard."

" Sir,—People in England, whatever political party they belong to, should glance at what is now going on in the town of Tipperary before finally making up their minds to hand over Ireland body and soul to the National League. No country town in Ireland—I think I may add or in England either—was more prosperous three months ago than Tipperary. The centre of a rich and prosperous part of the country, surrounded by splendid land, it had an enormous trade in butter and all agricultural produce, and a large monthly pig and cattle fair was held there. It possessed (I use the past tense advisedly) a number of excellent shops, doing a splendid business, and to the eyes of those who could look back a few years it was making rapid progress in prosperity every year.

" All is changed now. Many of the shops are closed and deserted, others will follow their example shortly ; the butter market has been removed from the town, the cattle fairs have fallen to half their former size. One sees shopkeepers, but a short time back doing capital business, walking about idle in the streets, with their shops closed ; armed policemen at every corner are necessary to prevent a savage rabble from committing outrages, and many people avoid going near the town at all. All this is the result of William O'Brien's speech in Tipperary and the subsequent action of the National League. The town and whole neighbourhood were perfectly quiet till one day Mr. O'Brien descends on it like an evil spirit, and tells the shopkeepers and surrounding farmers that they are to dictate to their landlords how to act in a case not affecting them at all. For fear, however, of not sufficiently arousing them for the cause of others, he suggests that, in addition to dictating to the landlord what his conduct shall be elsewhere, all his tenants, farmers and shopkeepers alike, shall demand a reduction of 25 per cent. on their own rents. As to the farmers' reduction I will say nothing ; if they wished it, they could go into the Land Court, and if rented too high could get a reduction, retrospectively from the day their application was lodged. The reduction, however, that the shopkeepers were advised—nay, ordered—to ask for must have surprised them more than their landlord. Many of them, at their existing rents, had piled up considerable fortunes in a few years ; others had enlarged their premises, doubled their business, and thriven in every way ; nevertheless, they had to obey. The landlord naturally refused to be dictated to by his tenants in matters not affecting them ; he also refused to reduce the rents of men who in a few years had made fortunes, and some of whom were commonly reputed to be worth thousands. Legal proceedings were then commenced, and the tenants' interests were put up to auction. Some of the most thriving shopkeepers declined to let their tenancies, out of which they had done so well, be sold ; others, in fear of personal violence and outrage, not unusual results of disobeying the League, did allow them to be knocked down for nominal sums to the landlord's representative. Let lovers of liberty and fairplay watch what followed. All the shopkeepers who bought in their interests were rigorously boycotted ; men who had had a large weekly turnover now saw their shops absolutely deserted. Plate-glass windows that would not have shamed Regent Street, were smashed to atoms by hired ruffians of the League, and the shopkeepers themselves and their families had to be protected from the mob by armed police, placed round their houses night and day. All this because they desired to keep their flourishing businesses, instead of sacrificing them in a quarrel not their own.

" Let us follow still further what happened. The shopkeepers, finding their trade quite gone, for it was almost worth a person's life to go into their shops, watched as they were by paid spies, had to capitulate to the League. An abject apology and a promise to let themselves be evicted next time were the price they had to pay to be allowed in a free country to carry on their trade. Ruin faced them both ways. After having the ban of boycotting taken off them, with eviction not far distant, most of them held clearance sales, at tremendous sacrifices, so as to be prepared for moving. One man is reputed to have got rid of seven thousand pounds' worth of goods under these circumstances. Of the other division, who allowed their places to be sold, most of them are now evicted. Dozens of shop assistants, needlewomen, and others connected with the trade of a thriving town, are thrown out of employment, and a peaceful neighbourhood has been changed into a scene of bloodshed and violence.

" I appeal to the English people not to encourage or support a vile system of intimidation and violence, a system which not only pursues and ruins its enemies, but refuses to allow peaceably-inclined people to remain neutral. A case like this should not be one of Party politics, but should be looked upon as the cause of all who wish to pursue their lawful vocations peaceably against those who wish to tyrannise by terror over the community at large.

" I am, Sir, your obedient servant,

" FŒDI FŒDERIS ADVERSARIUS."

" December 12."

My private letters strengthen and confirm every word of this account ; and the following letter is again a proof of personal tyranny and political malevolence not reassuring as qualities in the governing power :—

"TO THE EDITOR OF THE ' TIMES.'

" Sir,—I have received a letter from my friend Mr. Edward Phillips, of Thurlesbeg House, Cashel, and the round, unvarnished tale that he delivers throws more light upon Ireland than any amount of the windy rhetoric which is so plentifully displayed on Parnellite and Gladstonian platforms. Mr. Phillips writes as follows :—

" ' I hold 270 acres from Mr. Smith-Barry at a rent of £340 under lease and tenant-right, which, with my improvements, I valued at £1,000. The Land League have decided, thinking to hurt Mr. Smith-Barry, that all tenants must prepare to give up their farms by allowing themselves to be evicted. They are clearing off everything, and because I refuse to do this, and forfeit my £1,000, I am boycotted in the most determined manner. I am refused the commonest necessaries of life, even medicine, and have to get all from a distance.

Blacksmiths, &c., refuse to work, and labourers have notice to leave, but have not yet done so.

" ' Heretofore people were boycotted for taking farms; I am boycotted for not giving up mine, which I have held for 25 years. A neighbour of mine, an Englishman, is undergoing the same treatment, and we alone. We are the only Protestant tenants on the Cashel estate. The remainder of the tenants, about 30, are clearing everything off their land, and say they will allow themselves to be evicted.'

" I think this requires no comment. Public opinion is the best protection against tyranny, and your readers can judge how far the above narrative is consistent with the opinions expressed by Mr. Parnell and others as to the liberty and toleration which will be accorded to the loyal minority when the Land-National League becomes the undisputed Government of Ireland.

' Your obedient servant,

" R. BAGWELL."

" Clonmell, December 27th."

Again an important extract :—

" This is Mr. Parnell's language at Nottingham, but would he venture to use the same arguments in this country? Would he enumerate clearly to an Irish audience the countless advantages they derive from Imperial funds and Imperial credit, and tell them that the first step to Home Rule is the sacrifice of all these advantages? Our great system of national education is provided out of Imperial funds to the extent of about a million a year ; so are the various institutions for the encouragement of science and art which adorn Dublin and our other large towns. The Baltimore School of Fishery and other technical training places, the piers and harbours on the Irish Coast, the system of light railways, and the draining of rivers and reclamation of waste lands, are all supported out of the Imperial Exchequer. The Board of Works alone has been the medium of lending almost five millions of money on. easy terms under the Land Improvement Acts in the country. Nor have the agricultural interests been neglected. For erecting farmhouses alone over £700,000 has been given, while immense sums have been spent in working the Land Acts. For drainage over two millions have been lent, and a sum of over one million has been remitted from the debt. A debt of eight and a-half millions appears in the last return as outstanding from the Board of Irish Public Works, besides three millions and a-half from the corresponding board in England. In fact, there is not a project enumerated by Mr. Parnell as necessary, under a new *régime*, to promote the ' Nationality of Ireland,' which is not at present being helped on by the funds or the credit of the 'alien Government.' All these national advantages the supporter of a shadowy Home Rule bids us give up."

If ever there was a case of the spider and the fly in human affairs this mild and perfectly equitable reasoning of Mr. Parnell is the illustration. How about the djinn crying inside the sealed jar, and the fate of the

credulous fisherman who obeys that voice and breaks
the seal which Solomon the Wise set against him?

In writing this pamphlet I have not cared for graces
of literary style or dramatic strength of composition; and
I have largely supported myself by quotations as a proof
that I am not a mere impressionist, but have a solid
back-ground and a firm foothold for all that I have
said. Judged by these extracts it would seem that,
outside the right of full communal self-government, the
cry for Home Rule is either interested and fictitious—
or when sincere—save in certain splendid exceptions,
of whom Mr. Laing is the honoured chief, and the
only Home Ruler who makes me doubt the rightness
of my own conversion—it is a mere sentimental impulse
shorn of practical power and working capacity. In any
case it is a one-sided thing, leaving out of court Ulster, the
integrity of the Empire, and the obligations of historic
continuity. It is a cry that has been echoed by violence
and murder, by outrage and ruin, and that has in it one
overwhelming element of weakness—exaggeration. It
is the cry at its best of enthusiasts whose ideas of
human life and governmental potentialities are too
generous for every-day practice—at its worst but
another word for self. For the men who raise it and
hound on these poor dupes to their own destruction are
men who would be rulers of the country in their own
persons, or members of a Gladstonian ministry, were
the Home Rule party to come to the front. With
neither section does the strength, the glory, the
integrity, and the continuance of the Empire count;

and the honour of England, like the true well-being of Ireland, is the last thing thought of by either party. The motto of the one is: " *Fiat justitia ruat cælum* "—of the other: " *Apres moi le déluge.*" The one abjures the necessities of statesmanship, the other the self-restraints of patriotism. Surely the good, wholesome, working principles of sound government lie with neither, but rather with the steady continuance of things as they are—modified as occasion arises and the needs of the case demand.

MESSRS. METHUEN'S LIST.

BY THE AUTHOR OF "MEHALAH," "JOHN HERRING," &c.

Now ready at all Libraries.

ARMINELL: A SOCIAL ROMANCE.

3 vols.   Crown 8vo., 31s. 6d.

" There is shrewdness of observation and appreciation of the humorous side of human nature in Mr. Baring Gould's new novel."—*Athenæum.*

" It is not often that there appears so thoroughly entertaining a work."—*Graphic.*

By the SAME AUTHOR.

OLD COUNTRY LIFE: By S. BARING GOULD,

M.A. With Numerous Illustrations and Initial Letters by W. Parkinson, F. D. Bedford, and F. Masey. Large Crown 8vo., 10s. 6d. A Limited Edition on Large Paper has also been printed, 21s. net.

CONTENTS :—Chaps. 1. Old Country Families.—2. The Last Squire.—3. Country Houses.—4. The Old Garden.—5. The Country Parson.—6. The Hunting Parson.—7. Country Dances.—8. Old Roads.—9. Family Portraits.—10. The Village Musician.—11. The Village Bard.—12. Old Servants.—13. The Hunt.—14. The County Town.

" Bright, cheery and picturesque. No man knows or loves quaint old England better than Mr. Baring Gould. This delightful volume is illustrated with clever and comical drawings."—*Times.*

" Oddity, originality, and a feeling for locality are qualities of Mr. Baring Gould's mind and style, and in describing the lives and ways of the occupants of West Country manor houses and parsonages in the olden time, he can fairly revel in the odd and the original. The book is beautifully illustrated, and the design of the binding is itself a quaint and tasteful work of art."—*Scotsman.*

By the SAME AUTHOR.

HISTORIC ODDITIES AND STRANGE EVENTS. By S. BARING GOULD, M.A. Demy 8vo., 10s. 6d.

" A collection of exciting and entertaining chapters. The whole volume is delightful reading."—*Times.*

" The stories are well retailed, with admirable conciseness and point."—*Athenæum.*

By the SAME AUTHOR.

SONGS OF THE WEST: Traditional Ballads

and Songs of the West of England, with their Traditional Melodies. Collected by S. BARING GOULD, M.A., and H. FLEETWOOD SHEPPARD, M.A. Arranged for Voice and Piano. In 4 Parts (containing 25 Songs each), 3s. each net.   [*Parts I. and II. now ready.*

" A rich and varied collection of humour, pathos, grace, and poetic fancy."—*Saturday Review.*

By MAJOR N. PAUL.

ALDERDENE. By MAJOR NORRIS PAUL. Crown 8vo., 3s. 6d.

"A very remarkable story, which is sure to attract attention."—*Newcastle Chronicle.*

"Interesting, not to say fascinating."—*Birmingham Gazette.*

By A. M. M. STEDMAN, M.A.

OXFORD: ITS LIFE AND SCHOOLS. Edited by A. M. M. STEDMAN, M.A., assisted by members of the University. *New Edition, re-written.* Crown 8vo., 5s.

"We can honestly say of Mr. Stedman's volume that it deserves to be read by the people for whom it is intended, the parents and guardians of Oxford students, present and to come, and by such students themselves."—*Spectator.*

By THE AUTHOR OF "DONOVAN," "WE TWO," &c.

DERRICK VAUGHAN, NOVELIST. By EDNA LYALL. Post 8vo., 2s. 6d. Twenty-fifth Thousand.

"Edna Lyall has not written anything more artistic, or, from the moral point of view, more stimulating. In substance as well as in form, it is the manliest of Edna Lyall's books."—*Academy.*

By P. H. DITCHFIELD, M.A.

OUR ENGLISH VILLAGES: Their Story and their Antiquities. By P. H. DITCHFIELD, M.A., F.R.H.S., Rector of Barkham, Berks. Post 8vo., 2s. 6d., Illustrated.

"A pleasantly written little volume, giving much interesting information concerning villages and village life."—*Pall Mall Gazette.*

"An extremely amusing and interesting little book, which should find a place in every parochial library."—*Guardian.*

EDITED by F. LANGBRIDGE, M.A.

BALLADS of the BRAVE: Poems of Chivalry, Enterprise, Courage, and Constancy, from the Earliest Times to the Present Day. Edited with Notes, by REV. F. LANGBRIDGE. Crown 8vo., gilt edges, 5s.

"A very happy conception happily carried out. These 'Ballads of the Brave' are intended to suit the real tastes of boys, and will suit the taste of the great majority. It is not an ordinary selector who could have so happily put together these characteristic samples. Other readers besides boys may learn much from them."—*Spectator.*

"Mr. Langbridge's main object is to produce a volume that will please boys, and in this he has probably succeeded."—*Athenæum.*

"This charming volume is a healthy book for boys, including old boys."—*Echo.*

www.ingramcontent.com/pod-product-compliance
Lightning Source LLC
Chambersburg PA
CBHW021525270326
41930CB00008B/1099